50 Shades of Organizing . . . Your Life

Susan Unger

Lauri Mennel

50

Shades of Organizing

...Your Life

THE
Organazm Ladies
GET ORGANIZED. RELAX MORE.

Susan Unger

& Lauri Mennel

50 Shades of Organizing...Your Life

Copyright 2015 by Susan Unger and Lauri Mennel

Published in the United States by SassyLass Press.

ISBN 978-0-9864214-0-2
ISBN 978-0-9864214-1-9

Editor: Katherine Gotthardt
Designer: Glen Edelstein
Logo Designer: Donna A. Cregar

Author Photographer: Emily Korff, Veralana Photography

Even though I'm not allowed in his home office, my wonderful, supportive husband is always there for me. And to my newly married daughter who now asks for my organizing advice – something must've sunk in over the years.

Susan

To my incredibly smart, hard-working husband who still has to search for his keys most mornings and our adventurous, creative tween daughter who "gets" what I do but has absolutely no interest in following in my footsteps, today or ever.

Lauri

Acknowledgements

There are many people who helped us through the process of writing our first book. Katherine Gotthardt of All Things Writing was a fabulous editor, helping to make sure our words matched our message. Glen Edelstein of Hudson Valley Book Design was the super creative genius behind our cover and book design, as well as our website construction.

We also want to thank Kristie Brown Allen for her preview reading and editing, and to fellow author Kelly McDermott Harman for her generous sharing of advice on what it takes to publish a book. Joyce Leege, CPA of Moer & Leege, P.A. made sure we didn't overreach on any accounting tips. And we have to give a big shout out to Emily Korff at Veralana Photography for making us look simply fabulous!

And finally, we want to give a huge and heartfelt thank you to our wonderful clients. We learn from you every time we meet and hope that our work together has enabled you to live your best life.

Table of Contents

Contents

CONTENTS

50 Shades of Organizing . . . Your Life

Introduction

Or-ga-nazm /or' gan az um/ _n._ 1 the total bliss experienced in the midst of getting organized. **2** the climax of completing an organizing task or project.

Welcome to our world! We're The Organazm Ladies, and we're here to help you get a little more control over your life. Doesn't that sound lovely? We are two experienced professional organizers who are excited about spreading our love of organizing without scolding, without shame and without judgment. Honey, we've seen it all! We know that smart, capable women (and men) sometimes just need a little inspiration and confidence building to help them create the life they envision for themselves.

Reading _50 Shades of Organizing...Your Life_ will take you through a journey of fun and easy ideas that will make you feel great! We will share philosophies, tips, ideas and methods that we've seen work time and time again with our clients.

Use this book in whatever way makes sense to

you. Read through quickly to get an overall feel for our organizing philosophies. Search for a topic aligning to a problem area in your home. Close your eyes and pick a page! There is no right or wrong way to approach getting organized.

We have lots of favorite products, websites and other resources that we mention throughout the book. You can find the latest and greatest of these on our website, www.50ShadesOfOrganizing.com.

We don't promise getting organized is better than sex. But we do think you'll love the feeling you get when you have an organazm on a regular basis!

1. Cost of Disorganization

Have you ever thought about what disorganization *costs* you? Not just money, but time and peace of mind?

M O N E Y :

Late charges for past due bills.
Rush shipping charges for gift orders.
Buying duplicate items because you can't find something.

T I M E :

Time spent looking for car keys.
Time spent looking for phones.
Time spent looking for important documents.

PEACE OF MIND:

Have I paid that bill?
When do I need to turn in that report?
Have I responded to that request?

Recognizing that there are real costs involved in disorganization can often be the first step in making a change in your habits. Operating in crisis mode is very stressful to you and your relationships, both personal and professional.

Enough Negative Nellie talk! What are the positives of getting more organized? Taking control of your environment, your time and your stuff is a sure path to minimizing the stress in your life. It can make you more productive and give you more time for fun. Getting more organized will definitely save you money. Oh, and did we mention less stress?

Getting Started is the Hardest Part

You've decided you want to simplify your life. You know you have a lot of "stuff" that you don't need and don't really even want. You see articles and websites and books about organizing your life. And the thought of attaining such a peaceful and relaxing environment makes you sigh.

You are tired of wasting time and money and energy on looking for stuff. You are sick of looking at piles of paper or books or clothing that are meaningless to you.

But where do you start?

Start small and start detached. Clothes carry a lot of emotional weight, so you may not want to start with your closet. Instead, clear off a kitchen counter that has become a catch-all for random clutter.

Reward yourself. Organizing can be hard work, physically and emotionally. Take before and after pictures. Put them where you can see them and pat yourself on the back for a job well done.

Once you start, getting organized often leads to more organizing. When you experience the "aha!" moments, the contentment of knowing where stuff is and the beauty and efficiency of a well-organized home, you begin to really see how the time you spend organizing can truly change your life.

Let your vision of *how you want your life to be* guide you in this process. Just start.

3.
Ready, Set, GOAL!

Goal setting is perhaps the cornerstone of getting organized. The more clarity you have about how you want to live your life on a daily basis and where you want your life to go, the easier it is to make the time, space and energy needed to get organized. Your goals will drive your actions and decision-making will become easier while you are organizing.

Think of goal setting as structured dreaming. There are numerous goal-setting acronyms, but our favorite is SMART.

SPECIFIC

"I want to organize my home office" is too broad. "I want to be able to pay all of my bills on time" is specific. Let's see if that goal fits the rest of the SMART acronym.

MEASUREABLE

You can easily measure if you are paying your bills on time by creating a system to document when bills are due and when they've been paid.

ATTAINABLE

Paying bills on time is an attainable goal with the right systems in place.

REALISTIC

If you are not financially overextended, it is realistic that you can pay your bills on time.

TIMED

Each month, you will be able to ascertain whether or not you've met your goal of paying your bills on time.

If you don't meet a particular goal, don't beat yourself up! Take a look at what happened, tweak your system and try again. Always reward yourself for progress.

4. *Make the Time*

Whether this is the first organizing book you've read or the tenth, somewhere deep inside you crave the order and peace that you feel may come with a more organized life.

If living a life that is more relaxing and less stressful is one of your goals, then take the time to create the environment to support that goal. You have to believe that you are worth the time and effort. And it *will* take effort. And time. It will also take a willingness to change behavior and to adopt new strategies.

Making the time to prioritize yourself is also a way to take control of your stuff. Put organizing time on your calendar and treat it like a very important appointment with yourself. Again, this is a way to avoid living by crisis management. Yes, stress is part of being alive. It drives us to do better and to do more. But there is a happy medium. Becoming more organized will enable you to not sweat the small stuff.

5.

Help I Need Somebody!

Let's imagine for a moment that you've carved out 30 minutes to organize your junk drawer.

Then your phone rings. Your email pings. Facebook is beckoning. How many times do you find something else to do when you try to organize?

You might need a body double! That's what we professional organizers call another warm body who can help keep you on track during your organizing project.

Sometimes a body double is in the same room as you, maybe working on their own project and simply providing you with moral support. Other times your body double is right there in the trenches with you, helping you to make the hard decisions.

Try to recruit a non-judgmental friend or family member to hang out with you while you organize. Or you can hire a professional organizer to help you. Check out www.NAPO.net to find a professional organizer in your area.

It's OK to ask for help.

6.
Set the Stage for Success

Feeling good helps you do good work. Much of organizing, like any other project or job, depends on your mood and how you feel about the task at hand. If you are tired, hungry or just plain grumpy, you're probably not going to accomplish much that you set out to do.

For example, many of us identify as being a morning person or a night owl – a lark or an owl in the modern parlance. When is your energy level the highest? When are you most alert and feel the most productive? When is your mood the most positive?

If you are a lark, try to schedule an organizing task in the morning, perhaps after you've read the paper and had your two cups of coffee.

More of an owl? You'll get a lot more work done in

the late afternoon or evening when your energy level is high and your mood is good.

Do you like to work or play to music? Your favorite Pandora station, a beloved iPod mix or a podcast catch-up session can all richly enhance your productivity. Or maybe dead silence is music to your ears.

Whatever lifts your mood can often make work more fun and quicken your pace. And that can make all the difference in the world when you are in decluttering mode!

7

One Step at a Time

Be gentle with yourself when you make a commitment to get organized.

The clutter did not form in a day. It won't go away in a day.

But you can make headway by breaking up seemingly insurmountable projects (kitchen chaos anyone?) into smaller tasks that you can easily accomplish and feel good about your progress.

Here is an example of a kitchen fix that could take several days or a few weekends doing one step at a time:

Step 1: Clean out fridge.
Step 2: Declutter countertops.
Step 3: Tidy up under sink area.
Step 4: Organize pantry.

Step 5: Sort and purge plastic containers.
Step 6: Refresh junk drawer.

There. Doesn't that seem more realistic?

 HOT TIP

Here's a fun way to envision a doable task: take a peek through a paper towel tube at an area to be organized like your desk or a kid's room. Only deal with what you can see, ignoring everything else. It's a good way to literally see just a small part of a big job!

8.

SEXY Time

Here is our devastatingly simple and memorable method to organize everything from your purse to any room in your home: SEXY Time!

Here's an example using SEXY Time for a closet project.

S IS FOR SORT

Sorting is simply placing like items with like items. You need to see what you have before you can make decisions on what to do with any given category. Some natural sorting categories in a closet are pants, shirts, dresses, suits, belts, scarves, shoes, socks, sweaters and purses.

E IS FOR EXIT

From your sorting, you discover nine pairs of black pants! Oh my! Now you can make an intelligent decision on exactly how many pairs of black pants one really needs to get by in this world. Give the others a graceful exit from your home and your life through donating, consigning or even giving them to a friend.

X MARKS THE SPOT

After you've streamlined your clothing, shoes and accessories, take a look at how much you have of each category. It's time to assign the right size and spot for them in your closet. Use organizing tools to help make the most of your spots. Shelf dividers are hard-working tools to keep stacks of sweaters from tumbling on to each other. A nice basket on the floor of your closet can catch dry cleaning. Beautiful fabric boxes can corral small items like socks and tights.

Y IS FOR YAY! KEEP IT UP!

Ahhhh. Feel that Zen-like calm as you look at your newly cleaned and organized closet? Keep that feeling of Nirvana by regularly having SEXY time in your closet. Regular maintenance of newly organized spaces is the secret to keeping things under control. Try our SEXY Time technique with your purse, your kitchen pantry, your garage or any area that needs a little help.

9. Love, Beauty, Utility

So how exactly can we define clutter? Simply put, clutter is something that we don't love, need or want.

Clutter can also indicate decision avoidance. It's easier to NOT do something at all rather than to take the time and energy to figure out a plan of action. *Deciding to decide* can be a true paradigm shift in thinking.

As you are embracing your new organizing mindset of "less is more," ask yourself these three questions about each item you are considering:

Do I love it?
Is it beautiful?
Is it useful?

If you can't answer "yes" to at least one of these questions, then ask yourself if it's possible this item is clutter. If so, can you let it go? Also, ask yourself if this item is providing a benefit to you and helping you meet the vision you have for your life. If not, can you let it go?

10. Balancing Act

To create balance in your life requires two things.

1. Stop bringing so much stuff into your life.

This can apply to paper, stuff and commitments. Use the strategies in this book to lessen the amount of paper coming into your home. Chapter 36 is particularly helpful with this challenge! Be more mindful when shopping, asking yourself if you really need that third pair of black boots. Susan often advises her clients to walk away for 15 minutes or so before actually making a purchase decision. It gets easier to say "no" the more often you say it.

2. Let go of more stuff.

Often the hardest part of letting go of stuff is making the decision to actually let it go. Decide to decide. Let go of magazine subscriptions you don't read anymore. Let go of clothes that don't fit or don't make you feel gorgeous. Let go of broken items that will never be repaired. Let go of that committee assignment that doesn't bring you joy.

Develop these habits and equilibrium WILL happen!

HOT TIP

One of our go-to strategies to help our clients create balance in their lives is the "one in, one out" rule.

When you bring something new into your home, make sure you plan on letting go of something in the same category. For example, when you buy a new pair of shoes, take a good, hard look at your shoe collection and let one pair go into your donation bin.

11

What's Really Driving You Crazy?

Close your eyes and ask yourself what area of your home makes your stomach tighten up most when you walk in the door. We all have them. The kitchen countertop, the coat closet, the junk drawer, the coffee table, the entryway floor that just drives us absolutely crazy! It's stressful just looking at these areas and their clutter. So you don't. But the clutter doesn't go away.

Set a timer for 30 minutes, turn on some music and focus on just this one spot. See what you can accomplish with a trash bag, a recycling bag, a bag for donations and a "belongs somewhere else in the house" box.

You might be surprised.

What's really interesting is that some of our clients tell us that once they start organizing the hard stuff, organizing the easy stuff becomes, well, a lot easier. Other clients need to start with the low-hanging fruit to get into the organizing groove and *then* tackle the hard stuff.

HOT TIP

We love the Time Timer. It's a very unique time keeping tool for adults and kids. You can find more about it on our website.

Perfection Isn't Pretty

Have you ever had something on your to-do list that you just kept moving to the next day, then the next week, then the next month? Have you ever stared at your "junk room," shuddered, closed your eyes and just shut the door?

If so, you may be suffering from perfectionism! Perfectionism in this sense is the inability to even start a task due to the mindset, perhaps subconsciously, that if you can't do something perfectly, you simply won't try to do it at all!

Give yourself permission to be imperfect. We all are! Reward yourself for progress rather than perfection.

One of the most important pieces of advice we give to our clients is:

Perfection is the enemy of the good enough.

Let go of perfection. It will tie you down – and not in a good way!

13.
Just Say No

Many of our clients are Very Busy People. It's the world we live in. Many of us are tugged in numerous directions. But what does being "crazy busy" have to do with organizing?

Lots of us find it hard to set boundaries on our time, space and relationships. We don't want to disappoint. We put our own needs last. And then we wonder why we are running on empty much of the time.

It's time to give yourself permission to utter a very simple word. "No." You will not be judged. You will not be found "less than." You will not become friendless or a bad mom.

What you will gain by saying "no" is:

- **More heart space to give your children and significant others.**

- **More time to devote to the projects that will help you fulfill your life's vision.**
- **More energy to take care of yourself.**

Keep your "no" simple and concrete. When you give a wishy-washy "no," people think you are interested and will continue to press you.

Banish the guilt that comes with saying "no." You do not owe any explanations.

You may have a hard time saying "no" if your sense of self-worth depends on being indispensable. Value yourself. Don't feel the need to create value to others by overextending yourself.

Minimize your stress and be selective about where you spend your time and energy.

Decide to say "no."

14. Watch Out for Zigzag Organizing

When decluttering a room, you are invariably going to run across items that belong elsewhere in your home.

But running around putting things away in the middle of an organizing project offers so many potential distractions. "Oh, look! I need to put these clothes in the dryer." "Ha ha! I'll just take a quick peek at this funny cat video someone posted on Facebook!" "Those plants sure look like they need some water."

To avoid getting distracted or just wearing yourself out, don't worry about putting things away as you come across them.

Instead, keep a box or bin labeled "Belongs Somewhere Else" in the area you are organizing. Then periodically take the box around your home and put items in their proper place.

15.

K.J.S.S.

Keep It Super Simple. The simpler you keep a system, the easier it is to set up and, more importantly, to maintain.

There is a tendency for many of us to think that the more complex a system, the better it is. Sometimes having this mindset can send us down the perfectionism spiral (see Chapter 12) and nothing gets done!

Here are two examples of Keeping It Super Simple to organize what can often bog down even the most organized among us – paper and clothes.

• Keep one file folder or box labeled "Current Year Tax Information." Every time something tax-related comes across your desk, drop it in the file or box. When tax time comes along, guess what sharp cookie has all her paper ducks in a row and gets her tax return filed on time? Not to mention her refund back in record time! Yes, that would be you, darling!

• Keep a basket or bag in your closet. When you put on an item of clothing that just doesn't make you feel fabulous anymore, toss it in the bag. When the bag is full, take it to a local charity so someone else can have the chance to feel fabulous wearing it!

Remember to K.I.S.S. whenever you are implementing a new organizing system or process for your home. Why make things harder than they need to be? That's no fun!

16. Touch and Go

Overwhelmed with important papers and files? Have you got the junk mail toss down cold but get stumped by how to organize the papers and files you *do* need to keep?

Here's our touch technique to the rescue! We like to suggest simply assigning a "touch" time frame to any given file or information category that you have. For example, keep files that you touch at least monthly in an easily accessible spot at your desk like a nearby file drawer or desktop file. These might include items like your bill paying file, car repair file, upcoming travel documents, insurance claim forms and current year tax information file.

Now create an archive filing drawer or box that houses information and files that you might need to touch at least yearly or perhaps never again (but you just have to keep). Your archive might include things like past year tax returns and closing documents for your home purchase.

There is a lot of other great information on paper retention in Chapter 34. Check it out!

17.

Take 5 Every Day

Not many of us have the luxury of being able to spend an entire day on an organizing project. As we've discussed, you can and should break up projects into manageable blocks of time. Remember that perfection is the enemy of the good enough! It's better to knock out 30 minutes of decluttering when you have a little time rather than just throw your hands up in despair!

But how about just five minutes? Can a five-minute habit really make a difference in your life? Here are some super quick daily habits you can start that will reward you handsomely for the small amount of time they take:

- **Make your bed.**
- **Clear off your bathroom counter.**
- **Fold a basket of clothes.**
- **Empty trash from your car.**

- **Unload the dishwasher.**
- **Toss out refrigerated food past its prime.**
- **Clean out your purse.**
- **Quick sort your mail.**
- **Clear your desk.**
- **Toss dirties in the hamper.**

HOT TIP

Work on one five-minute habit at a time until it develops into a true habit. Progress is your goal!

18.
Feed the Monster!

W ho says professional organizers can't learn from their clients? One of Lauri's clients introduced her to "feeding the monster!" It's a fantastic way to keep on top of getting stuff out of your house, stuff that you no longer need, love or want.

Here's how it works:

Keep donation containers in various parts of your home. These containers, or monsters, can be small boxes, grocery bags or bins. "Feed the monster" regularly with items you run across that you no longer wear, enjoy or need. Once a month, take it away to your favorite charity. Love those tax deductions! And getting stuff out of your home will always have you feeling light as a feather!

Strange but true, don't be surprised if you start LOOKING for things to feed the monster. Ideal spots for monsters are closets, mudrooms, kitchen pantries, garages and kids' rooms.

19.
Money, Money, Money

Think you can make a few dollars off of some of your cast-off items? There are certainly ways to sell items if they are worth your time and energy. It's a good idea to mentally set a dollar threshold on what is worth your effort to sell. Something that will bring you $5.00 is simply not worth your valuable time!

We are not big fans of garage sales because they require SO MUCH WORK! However, if you have a lot of items, particularly furniture and other things that might bring in more than a few dollars, holding a garage sale might be worth your time.

If you don't mind strangers coming to your home, consider listing bigger ticket items on Craigslist.com. Check the listings in your area to see what certain items are fetching before you decide it's worth the hassle.

A good consignment store is often a great place to take gently worn, still-stylish clothing. Consignment stores usually focus on a single segment of the clothing market, for example, women's, men's or children's clothing and accessories. The store will take your pieces and give you 50% or so if the item sells.

eBay is also an option for selling. You can post your own eBay auction listings or use one of the many eBay auction houses or eBay "valets" that are out there. This requires more effort on your part – think high dollar items.

Become an Amazon.com Seller and earn money sitting at your desk! Find out how on Amazon.com.

HOT TIP

Commit to donating all items that you can't sell within a certain time frame. This helps keep your "inventory" from piling up and defeating the decluttering process.

20.
Safe Passage

Sometimes it's hard to let go of things. You paid a lot for that dress even though you've only worn it once and didn't really feel that good in it. Your best friend gave you that book that you've never read. Yes, you have accumulated five glass pie plates, but what if you need to make five pies? All at once?

One helpful way to ease the emotional chore of letting things go is to think about the eventual person who might end up with that item. We mean really, really think about that person. When you donate an item of clothing to a women's shelter, picture a woman selecting your dress to wear to the first interview she's had in years.

The book you have absolutely no interest in reading may spark a stranger's lifelong interest in the topic.

When you donate to a thrift store, you are allowing someone who couldn't afford to pay full price for an item the chance to wear or read or use something that was out of reach financially.

As you go through your purging process, really think about what you have and what you need. Then think about what others need that they may never have. This is also a great lesson to impart to your kids.

If you can close your eyes and envision someone else's joy at acquiring something that is just clutter to you, it begins to feel like you are offering a safe passage to that item. And that feels really, really good.

21.
Create Your Own Personal Strip Mall

How much time and energy do you spend searching for items on a daily basis? We stress to our clients that being organized is not a matter of living a minimalist existence. It's simply being able to put your hands on what you need, when you need it, with minimal fuss.

There are four categories of items that just beg to be stored together. We like to group them in a version of our own personal strip mall located right inside our homes!

• **My Best Buy:** Any computer peripherals, phone chargers, cable cords, back-up keyboards, headsets or other electronic odds and ends can be stored in one place, perhaps in a drawer in your home office or a bankers box in the basement.

- **My Container Store:** Do you have plastic bins, decorative tins, jars, boxes, magazine holders and baskets that would be perfect to corral "like with like" items? Great! Keep them all together. Then when you need a container, you'll be able to find just the right one. Store them in a closet or on a shelf in your basement or guest room.

- **My Home Depot/Lowe's:** Most of us have collected random household repair items over the years. Tape, clips, nails, hand tools, picture hanging supplies, glues, string/rope, gloves, sandpaper and light bulbs are just a few of the hundreds of things you might have around your home. Keeping them all together will allow you to find what you need when you need it. A small bookshelf or workbench in your garage or basement might be just the place for your Lowe's.

- **My Office Depot/Staples:** If it's an office supply or school supply, keep it together! A file drawer or kitchen cabinet works great for these supplies.

The beauty of your own personal strip mall is that you can tell an inquiring housemate, spouse or kid, "Oh, that's in Lowe's!" or "Yes, you can find that in Best Buy."

22. Like With Like

A basic mantra in the organizing world is to put "like with like." There is a certain mental calm that comes with knowing that all of your batteries are in one shoebox on the third shelf of the kitchen cabinet to the right of your refrigerator. If you don't believe us, try it!

The "like with like" method works with just about everything:

Light bulbs
Black pants
Extension cords
Keys
Candles
Travel size toiletries
Chip clips
Collar stays

Recipes

Flash drives

Bathing suits

Cheese knives

Hair brushes

Legos

Envelopes and postage stamps

Halloween decorations

Well, you get the idea!

HOT TIP

There are some categories that beg to be labeled. That box of light bulbs will be much more visible to everyone in your home if you have a big "Light Bulbs" label on the front of the container. This is important since you want to have everyone in the house on your maintenance team.

23.
Location, Location, Location

You know what they say in the real estate business: location is everything! The same can be said when you are deciding on where to place items in your home.

Whether you are working on your kitchen, your bathroom, your garage or a clothes closet, continually appraise items to determine whether they "deserve" a prime piece of real estate or can be stored in an area that is not so accessible.

Think about how often you need to use an item. Is it daily? Weekly? Once a year? Only use the most valuable real estate in your home for things you use very frequently.

When you are clearing out a cabinet in the kitchen, ask yourself, "Does this water bottle that I use on hikes a couple of times a year deserve to be in the same cabinet as the coffee cups I use every day?"

Each drawer, surface, shelf, closet, cabinet and room in your home has an intrinsic real estate value. Let location be top of mind when you are decluttering and organizing your space.

24. *Contain Yourself*

We love us some Container Store. And Target. And Bed Bath and Beyond. We could lose ourselves in the fabulousness of the latest color, fabric or pattern of containers to store all of our whatnots. And you could, too. But you don't have to.

Don't let a small-to-zero budget stop you from putting some basic organizing methods to work in your home. Remember, perfect is the enemy of the good enough!

- **First aid kits fit nicely into a shoe box.**
- **A cookie tin makes a great home for small office supplies.**
- **A gallon size Ziploc™ bag will whip those power cords into shape.**

- **Sturdy bankers boxes from office supply stores are super inexpensive and can be used for anything from files to sweaters.**

Another important thing to remember: don't go buy a bunch of organizing supplies until you know what you need. This is the single biggest mistake we see when we enter our clients' homes for the first time – loads and loads of organizing supplies! You need to do your SEXY Time before you can assess what type, size and number of containers you need.

Once you know what quantity and size of containers you need for a project, you can make it your mission to search your home and see if you have any containers that would work.

HOT TIP

If you do buy containers, try to stick with clear containers. It's so much easier to quickly assess what's inside when you can actually SEE it! If you go the decorative route with patterned or textured containers, make sure you can label the contents with a hanging tag or a sticky label.

25.

I Can See Clearly Now

Yes, a great song from the '70s, but also a reminder that seeing things clearly is helpful to many of us "visual people!"

Most of us do better finding things when we can SEE them! One great tool for collecting small to medium items in a collection is a clear, over-the-door shoe holder.

You can use this handy holder in so many places. It changes dead space – the back of a door – into fabulous space! Use one on your linen closet door to hold travel size toiletries. Use another in your mudroom or garage entry door to hold mittens, scarves and gloves in the winter, sunscreen, goggles and hats in the summer. You can also cut one to custom fit a cabinet shelf or narrow door.

And, of course, you can always use one on the back of your closet door. For shoes.

These shoe holders are an excellent example of using vertical space, an often overlooked wealth of real estate in our homes! Good use of vertical space might also mean:

- **Selecting a six-foot tall bookshelf instead of a three-foot tall bookshelf.**
- **Using a bulletin board near your desk to hold a task list, photos, invitations and other things that can clutter your desktop.**
- **Trying one of Susan's fave organizing tools – a pantry door rack. These are great to put on the interior of your pantry door. And it's super easy to install!**

It's gonna be a bright, bright...sunshiny day!

26.

Oh, Ziploc™ Bags, How I Love Thee!

Another *clearly* good idea is to use Ziploc™ bags for organizing. Ziploc™ bags can be one of the most useful tools to corral small or wayward items. They are clear, come in many sizes and are pretty darn sturdy, especially the freezer bags!

Here are some ideas on what to put in Ziploc™ bags:

- **Earbuds**
- **Power chargers**
- **Erasers**
- **Flash drives**
- **Stamps (remember those?)**
- **Ponytail holders and hair clips**

- **Extension cords**
- **Holiday gift tags**
- **Over-the-counter medicine "kit" supplies for when you travel**
- **Binder clips**
- **Coupons**

Can you think of others?

Once you've corralled these items in Ziploc™ bags, keep them in the spot you've designated as their home!

27.
Think Outside the Box

Reuse. Recycle. Repurpose. The three-legged stool of environmental mindfulness.

- Use a tissue box to store reusable plastic bags.
- Label those plastic bread bag tags and clip on to computer power cords for easy identification.
- Try placing a laundry basket or two in the trunk of your car to hold bags of groceries.
- Use an ice cube tray for earrings and rings or small craft supplies.
- Keep elastic hair ties neat and pretty on the outside of a toilet paper or paper towel roll.

**You can also tuck extension cords inside
these rolls to keep them under control.**

We love, love, love the regular feature in *Real Simple* magazine, "New Uses for Old Things." There is a fantastic roundup of their "50 All-Time Favorite New Uses for Old Things." Oh, my! Now that's an organazm-worthy article! Find it on our website.

28.
When Everything is Important, Nothing is Important

One of the most common reasons for our clients' inability to let go of something is that it has too many memories attached to it. Try repeating this mantra to help you figure out what's really important to save and what you can let go: when everything is important, nothing is important.

The artistic, creative and intellectual output of our children is a good example of how we physically attach to items that might eventually overwhelm even the most sentimental parent. Try taking photos of your children's creations and only keeping the very best representation of their work each year.

If you do a lot of traveling, you likely have souvenirs, maps, menus, playbills and other memorabilia that you've brought home along with great memories. Create a book using an online service like Shutterfly or Snapfish to capture all of the good times.

What are the *true* treasures among all of your collections? Keep those, photograph the rest and let your heart hold your memories!

 **HOT TIP**
This mantra also works when you are looking through the 11,286 photos on your computer (Lauri's dirty little secret). Don't hesitate to press that "delete" key!

29.
Beware of Flat Surfaces

We professional organizers call them "hotspots." Any area that seems to magnetically attract clutter and the detritus of daily life can be considered a hotspot.

They are most often flat surfaces. The floor right inside your front door, the kitchen counter where you plop your purse each night, and the dining room table that hasn't seen a meal in months are all likely culprits. Your car, your purse or your briefcase can also turn into a hotspot faster than you can say, "Now where is that check I need to deposit?"

Hotspots are hard! They require almost daily attention to keep them from devolving into a hot mess of paper, random objects and trash that belong nowhere near the hotspot.

If you have a hotspot or three (and most of us do),

add them to your five-minute habit list (see Chapter 17) and deal with them every day or two. Or use your steely willpower and try to overcome the habit of unthinkingly dropping items on to known hotspots. Baby steps will get you there!

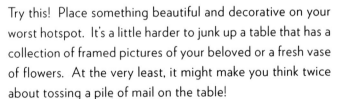

HOT TIP

Try this! Place something beautiful and decorative on your worst hotspot. It's a little harder to junk up a table that has a collection of framed pictures of your beloved or a fresh vase of flowers. At the very least, it might make you think twice about tossing a pile of mail on the table!

30.
Two Minute Rule

This organizing technique is so simple, we almost didn't put it in the book.

However, we've heard from so many of our clients that this one rule allows them to get stuff done that otherwise would've been sitting on their to-do list or on a sticky note on their bulletin board.

OK, here it is:

If you can do a task in two minutes or less, just do it.

- **RSVP to an invitation.**
- **Make that dentist appointment.**
- **Hang up your pants.**
- **File a paid bill.**
- **Put on a fresh roll of toilet paper.**

- **Call your best friend/mother/sister. Oh, wait. That will take A LOT longer than two minutes. Never mind.**
- **Wipe the crumbs off your kitchen counter.**
- **Take out the trash.**

31.
Use Your Brain for Dreaming

Do you have bits of paper scribbled with phone numbers, websites or things you want to do someday floating around your desk? Are there sticky notes on top of your sticky notes? Is your purse a repository of forgotten good intentions?

We tend to expend a lot of psychic energy in keeping track of the minutia of our lives. Books we want to read. Websites we want to visit. Bills we need to pay. Things we want to do. We call this "psychic clutter."

Try funneling and releasing all of this energy by using a simple spiral notebook with a fun, aesthetically pleasing cover to capture all the flotsam of your mind. Lauri calls this her "brain." *It's not a to-do list!* It's a brain dump of not-so-incredibly-important information, but stuff you might want to act on "one of these days."

Read about a website you want to visit someday? Jot it down. Hear from a friend about a fantastic book you want to read? Make a note. See a great gift idea while you are flipping through a catalog? Tear out the item and tape it into your notebook.

You'll be amazed at how freeing it is to get all the stuff floating around in your brain and on your desk into one place. You know it's there. You know you can access it when you want to or need to or have a moment of peace and quiet.

If you are completely paper-free, use this same concept on an app like Evernote, or just keep a running Excel spreadsheet of data.

Did we mention your "brain" is not a to-do list?

32.

3-2-1 Blast Off!
Or, "Houston,
We Have a Solution!"

Do your mornings consist of mad dashes throughout the house, looking for car keys, a permission slip or
library book? Is your cell phone dead? Are your kids in
a panic, searching for their homework or their gloves?
Hubby can't find his sunglasses?

You may find the key to a less-harried morning
routine is to add a launch and landing pad to your home's
most used entrance. It may be an area near your front
door or, if you're lucky, a nice, big mudroom.

Simply put, a launch and landing pad is a designated
area where routine items are placed upon entering
your home (the landing pad) and taken when leaving

(launching you out the door). There may be a closet near this area and, ideally, a table, a small wastebasket and hooks for bags, purses and backpacks.

Each family member should have his or her own basket or shelf to keep small items such as keys, cell phones, work badges and wallets. An outlet for charging phones is a big bonus. The ability for each family member to "grab and go" important items is key to keeping the morning chaos to a minimum.

For smoother mornings, get all members of the household into the habit of placing important items on the landing pad when they walk in the door. And, likewise, make sure that everything is in its place on the launch pad in the evenings. The more you can prepare the night before, the less stressful your mornings will be.

Everyone deserves to start off the day in a confident, relaxed state of mind!

33

To-Do Ta-Da!

One of the most important organizing habits we recommend embracing is the keeping of a to-do list. Although it seems like the punch line to a joke about the uber-organized, writing down all those tasks you need to do is a great way to save time, money and your sanity. Once you have jotted down an item on your to-do list, you can forget about it, freeing up your brain to dwell on more important things. Just the act of writing down tasks can make you more effective. Seriously.

The human brain loves a good "flow." You know that groove you feel when you are deep into a project or task? You feel enormously efficient and productive! Try playing to that groove by grouping similar tasks together when you create your to-do lists.

Carve out time each day or week to call those family and friends you still actually communicate with by phone. Likewise, set a time or two each day to attend to personal emails.

Do a quick pantry and fridge inventory during your routine meal planning and shopping time. Keep a box for clothing or household items that need to be taken in for alterations or repair.

Get into the habit of grouping errands together on your to-do list. You'll not only save gas, you'll save time that you can use for more enjoyable activities! Before you leave the house or office, think geographically about routing your errands so that your drive takes the least amount of time and mileage.

Pick a system for your to-do list that works for you.

- **Keep a pretty, small notebook in your purse. For many, there is great tactile satisfaction in crossing off a completed task.**
- **Use a simple 3x5 index card for your to-do list – it's the epitome of the K.I.S.S. method of to-do list making!**
- **Put each task on a sticky note and keep them all on a whiteboard, pulling them off when finished.**
- **Try one of the multitude of apps that**

function as to-do lists. Lauri uses an iPhone app called Errand. See our website for more resources for creating a to-do list system that works for you.

Can we share a little secret with you? We have both been known to add a task to our to-do list after the fact just to get that little thrill of crossing it off!

HOT TIP

Plan a specific time each year – your birthday is a good date – to make all of your annual medical and dental appointments. You'll never wonder again, "Huh, so when <u>was</u> my last mammogram?!"

34.
The Paper Toss

Paper is hard. There is just so much of it in our lives. Many people worry about tossing paper clutter because they think they might be throwing away something useful or important. So it's just easier to let the paper accumulate.

Here are some basic guidelines to help ease your mind! Our lawyer tells us that we must remind you that these are only guidelines. Check with your accountant or attorney to make sure these tips make sense with your specific financial situation.

TOSS OR SHRED EACH MONTH:

- **ATM receipts, bank deposit slips, sales receipts for minor purchases and credit card receipts (after making sure they match the statement).**

TOSS OR SHRED AT THE BEGINNING OF THE YEAR FOR THE PREVIOUS YEAR:

- **Paycheck stubs after you've reconciled them to your W-2.**
- **Monthly bank, brokerage or mutual fund statements.**
- **Mortgage statements as long as you receive a year-end statement showing your interest and property tax payments.**
- **Utility bills, unless you have a home office or need to prove residency.**

TOSS OR SHRED AFTER SEVEN YEARS:

- **Utility bills, if you have a home office or any other business related deduction.**
- **Any receipts or statements related to tax deductible expenses like childcare bills, out-of-pocket medical expenses, mortgage interest statements, etc.**

NEVER TOSS:

- Tax returns.
- Home improvement records.
- Receipts for big-ticket items (unless you get rid of it).
- Year-end statements from brokerage or financial services accounts.
- Confirmation records showing purchase price for any investments.

HOT TIP

Keep a small shredder and a wastebasket for recycling near your desk. Having the right tools close by makes it easier to keep the paper under control.

35.

Got Mail?

Mail has got to be one of the biggest issues for many of our clients. It has all the hallmarks of an organizing nightmare. It ruthlessly appears almost every day. Much of it is junk. Most of it needs a decision or an action.

Here is one strategy for beating back the beast.

Identify a dedicated spot to open your mail. Keep the following items there:

1. **A letter opener. The prettier the better.**
2. **A recycling bin.**
3. **A shredder or a "shred" basket.**
4. **A table to hold your glass of wine.**

Now, when you come into your home with your mail, go directly to your "Mail Spot." Put your mail on the table. Go pour a glass of wine. Go back to your Mail Spot. Open up each piece of mail with your pretty letter opener. Toss junk (including those annoying marketing inserts in your legitimate mail) into the recycling bin. Feed sensitive junk (we know, an oxymoron, but things like those "convenience checks" that your credit card company mails to you) into your shredder.

You've probably disposed of 80% of what was in your mailbox. Now, take the *real* mail, put it on your desk and deal with it.

- **Sort each piece into simple file categories like "Pay," "Action," "File" or "Read." Keep these "touch every day" files close at hand in a fun desktop file or a nearby file drawer.**
- **Mark your calendar with any time-sensitive actions needed.**
- **Add tasks to your to-do list.**

Now finish your glass of wine and pat yourself on the back.

36.
Just Stop the Damn Paper From Ever Getting to Your Mailbox!

Remember 10 or 15 years ago when all of us thought we would be "paperless" in the very near future? That didn't really pan out, did it?

So many people are overwhelmed by mail and paper. Here are three tasks that will dramatically cut down the amount of paper that ever hits your mailbox. And won't that just make it all so much simpler?

1. Go to a stop catalog website like http://www.catalogchoice.org. This website gives you options to stop all those unwanted catalogs from coming into your mailbox.

2. Ditto for this stop junk mail website: http://www.dmachoice.org. It might take a few weeks to notice a difference, but we promise you will reduce your junk mail by using this service.

3. Remember your "brain" notebook? That is a good place to keep a running list of businesses to change to "paperless" billing. This list would include bank statements, credit card statements, financial prospectuses, etc. Each time you have changed your delivery system from snail mail to email, cross the business off your list and enjoy one less piece of mail (or ten!) from coming into your home.

HOT TIP

They're not paper, but all those annoying telemarketing calls can also derail your time and efficiency. Sign up for the National Do Not Call Registry at http://www.donotcall.gov. Don't forget to also register your cell phone number!

37.
Piles and Piles of Magazines, Oh My!

A common thread among our clients who have accumulated piles of magazines is that they are saving them for one recipe or one article contained inside.

Here's a way to avoid this situation. As you are reading your favorite magazine and run across an interesting recipe, article or gift idea, tear the page out and circle the item. When you are finished with the magazine, you can toss it in the recycling bin. This will help you maintain your "one in, one out" process (see Chapter 10) with magazines.

Now, what to do with all of those lovely clippings?

- **Keep a "read" file on your nightstand or in your car.**

- **Create a "recipes to try" folder and keep it in your kitchen. If you haven't tried the recipe in a month or two, toss it. If the recipe is for a specific holiday or for entertaining, create a separate file.**
- **Start a "gift idea" folder. When your nephew's birthday rolls around, you won't be at a loss over what to get him. (See Chapter 42 for ideas on tracking the gifts you give.)**
- **Keep a folder for home decorating ideas.**
- **Use a folder for health and fitness tips you want to reference.**

You can use this same technique when you are perusing catalogs! Only tear out things of interest to you. Most catalog names can be found on each page, so you'll know the source without having to keep the entire catalog.

38.
Organizing as Child's Play

If you lead, they will follow. It's important to make organizing systems easy for children to maintain. Teach your children that everything has a home. Let them help decide where different toys "live." Give them input into purchasing or identifying containers to keep their toys. Have your kids participate at an early age in the purging process. This is the best way to teach them that it's OK to let things go.

Avoid deep toy boxes! They almost always become receptacles for lost and broken toys. Shallow is better.

Have your child label bins for various categories of toys. Legos, dolls, puzzles, action figures and balls are some common categories. If your kids are younger, let them draw pictures and tape the pictures onto containers.

Help get your kids into a regular routine of tidying up. Be specific and age appropriate in your directions and expectations.

Use clear containers so kids can actually see their treasures. Clear containers help kids choose what to play with and help them clean up later.

39

Master the Family Calendar

A time-proven solution for keeping all family members on top of everyone's activities is the Master Family Calendar. It's important to keep the calendar in a spot where everyone can see at a glance what is on tap for the day or week or month.

You can use a large, monthly paper calendar or mount a permanent whiteboard calendar that you re-create each month. The important thing is that everyone's activities go on the board as soon as they are known.

Parents' travel schedules, extracurricular activities, doctors' appointments, vacation days, birthdays and school holidays are just some of the events that affect the families' schedule and need to be known.

Now, what's the use of having this awesome calendar if no one ever looks at it? That's right. You also need to train yourself and your tribe to look at the calendar every morning and/or evening.

HOT TIP

It's fun and practical to use color-coded dry erase markers or pencils for each person's activities.

40.
Do You Know Where Your Owner's Manual Is?

Want an easy solution to keep track of all the various owner's manuals and instruction guides that float into our lives? You may have a warranty issue and need to find the receipt. Perhaps you are selling an item and want to include the instruction manual. Or maybe you just forgot how to set the time on your fancy running watch.

Collect and store all of your owner's manuals in one place.

- **Use part of a file drawer.**
- **Try a small portable file box to keep everything handy.**

- **Buy an accordion file with A to Z labels to keep things accessible alphabetically. Keep it in a closet or in a file cabinet drawer.**

When you purchase an electronic item, an appliance or anything you want to keep tabs on, staple the receipt to the front of the user guide and file it away. It'll be there if you need it!

Our one exception to this tip is to keep all of your small kitchen appliance manuals in the kitchen. Susan uses a small, three-ring binder with pocket pages to keep her kitchen appliance manuals handy. Keep the binder in a drawer or tucked inside a cabinet.

Be sure to toss old manuals when you no longer have the item. You can also thin out your owner's manual file once or twice a year.

HOT TIP

Can't find an instruction manual when you need one? Are you paper-free? Most owner's guides can be found online. Just Google the brand name and model number, and you'll likely find a PDF of the manual.

41.
Emergency Plan...STAT!

It may seem alarmist to think a real emergency could happen to us or our loved ones. Natural disasters, technological or accidental hazards, and terrorist hazards all seem unlikely to occur to us. But the more we are prepared for unlikely events, the less we will have to worry about them.

Formulating a family emergency plan is the cornerstone to an effective strategy that will leave your family feeling secure. A fantastic website that covers everything from A to Z is http://www.ready.gov. You can find very specific instructions on how to put together an effective emergency plan for your family, as well as emergency kits for your home and car.

It's also safe to say that none of us ever thinks there will be a fire in our home. However remote the possibility, it's a really, really good idea to have a firebox for your most important papers.

You can buy a small firebox at Office Depot or Staples for under $50. It will easily hold important documents like birth certificates, marriage licenses, Social Security cards, passports and other precious paperwork that would be a real pain in the ass to replace!

If you are comfortable and confident with cloud-based storage, you might also consider scanning copies of all of your important documents and sending them to a cloud storage system like Backblaze, Carbonite or iCloud.

42.

Drop the "Shop 'til You Drop"

Are you still buying goods for a household of three children, a husband, two cats and a dog, even though two of the kids are gone and living in their own homes (and maybe the husband, too)?

Shopping habits can become deeply ingrained. Buy for your current lifestyle. You'll save time, money and space.

There are many other ways to save time and money when it comes to shopping.

At first glance it may seem that grocery shopping online is an extravagance. However, think about how much impulse buying you do while cruising up and down the aisles. You may actually end up saving money if you shop for groceries online. And you can't beat doing your grocery shopping in your PJs at 10:00 p.m. with a glass of wine and no whining kids in sight! Hurray for Peapod.com!

The metaphorical two slices of bread that surround the "meat" of grocery shopping are meal planning and cooking ahead. It's a lovely feeling to know exactly what you are going to make for dinner each night of the week. We promise you'll save money and eat healthier as well, since you will not be tempted to throw in the towel during the 6:00 p.m. witching hour and order pizza. Again.

Keep a running shopping list in a visible area of your kitchen. Train other household members to add to the list when their favorite item is running low or they finish it off.

Spend 30 minutes or so every week planning what you'll have for dinner each night. Jot down any ingredients you don't have on hand and add to your shopping list. Then shop online or pick a time when your energy level is good and the grocery store is not crowded. Use your list and stick to it! And don't go to the store hungry!

Think about any items you can cook ahead or at least prep. Cooked pasta keeps very well in the fridge for a few days and is ready to go when you are. Have other family members help with chopping veggies to store in the fridge until ready to use. Cook extra chili, stews or spaghetti sauce and freeze for another time.

HOT TIP

Susan uses a nice, fresh envelope for her grocery list. She can then insert any coupons that she is using for that week's grocery shopping.

43.
It's Better to Give Than to Receive

Hmm, did I send Aunt Susie a birthday gift?

One way to reduce this "psychic clutter" is by keeping a spreadsheet to track all your annual gift giving. It's a wonderful planning and budgeting tool to make sure you have just the right gift for friends and loved ones. You can keep this spreadsheet right on your computer desktop or print it out and file it in your filing cabinet.

Make a list of friends and family members, along with a budget and the actual expense of their birthday and holiday gifts.

Don't forget to add Mother's and Father's Day, school graduations, anniversaries and any other gift-giving occasions you celebrate.

While we're talking about gift giving, keep a small, out-of-the-way area to store gifts that you pick up throughout the year. Often we see things that we think would be perfect for a friend or family member, but it's nowhere near their birthday or other gift-giving occasion. No worries. Just purchase and document the item on your gift list.

Also, don't let anyone tell you it's not cool to re-gift. It's perfectly acceptable to re-gift items that aren't really YOU but would be great for someone else! That is the epitome of re-purposing, right? Just make damn sure you don't re-gift something to the original giver! Not cool. This is a very preventable faux pas. Simply put a sticky note on the item with the name of the giver and keep it in your gift stash to use as a last minute gift.

Keep a file (either paper or electronic) called "Gift Ideas." As you come across neat gift ideas in magazines, newspapers and catalogs, clip them out and mark with the name of the potential recipient. See a great gift idea online? Jot it down and keep those notes in your "Gift Ideas" file.

HOT TIP

Get a greeting card organizer and pick up birthday cards as you find ones that fit the style and personalities of friends and family.

44. Tool Around

Whether your home is a one-story rambler with a basement or a three-story townhouse, it's super helpful to keep a basic tool kit on each floor of your home.

Use a small toolbox or even a shoebox to keep the following items close at hand:

Hammer
Slotted screwdriver
Phillips screwdriver
Pliers
Tape measure
Small variety of nails and screws
Picture-hanging hardware
Pencil

It's kind of amazing how often you will fix those nagging little home repairs if you don't have to go in search of the right tool!

- **Tighten a jiggly door knob.**
- **Hang that lovely picture.**
- **Remove old nails from the closet shelf.**
- **Sandpaper that rough stair step.**

Convenience is your friend.

HOT TIP

For the same reason it's also a good idea to keep a bucket of basic household cleaning supplies on each level of your home.

45.
Garage-A-Go-Go

Would you like to park a car or two in your garage? Is your garage a collection of delayed decisions, an "I don't know what to do with this thing so I'll just stash it in the garage" situation?

As you make plans to declutter and organize your garage, remember, aesthetics don't rule in the garage – functionality does!

There are six steps from a cluttered garage to one that you will enjoy using. Keep in mind that a garage is a big project! It's likely not a job that will take a few hours, but possibly even a few days! And remember, many hands make lighter work – ask for help.

1. Purge the low-hanging fruit. The broken lawn-mower. The little kid sports gear that your teenagers

haven't used in years. Trash. Random pieces of lumber. Old carpet remnants. Donate these items if they are in good shape. For bulky items that aren't donation worthy, call a junk hauler or your garbage company if they offer special pick-ups.

2. Identify the zones you want to have in your garage. The most common zones are tools; lawn and garden; sports and recreation equipment/bikes; trashcans and recycling bins; and seasonal items (think beach gear to holiday decorations).

3. Use the driveway as a staging area. Pull out and sort each item into its appropriate zone. Use cardboard boxes to temporarily corral items.

4. Take a good look at the contents of each zone and carefully think about the type and size of containers and other storage solutions you will need to wrangle them. Remember SEXY Time!

5. Give your garage a good sweeping. Place shelving units along walls. You can spend a little or a lot on shelves. You might want to install wall-mounted systems for hanging yard tools, mops and brooms, ladders and bikes. Ceiling mounted systems are great for canoes, kayaks and bikes. Our

suggestions for each of these organizing systems and tools can be found on our website.

6. Place items into their new homes and enjoy!

HOT TIP

Consider the weather carefully before planning your garage makeover. Spring and fall are nice seasons to be doing a garage project.

46.
Don't Get Freezer Burned!

Do you know what's in your freezer? Right now? If you're lucky, you reach in and pull out something that is potential dinner material. But if you are like many people, your freezer contents are a big mystery. Have you ever bought a bag of frozen peas or a family pack of chicken thighs because you didn't know you already had some in your freezer? Yep, we've been there, too.

Let's whip that freezer into shape! First things first. It sounds painful. It may seem overwhelming. But it's got to be done. Empty your freezer. Yes, take everything out. Have a few supplies at hand: a trashcan, a Sharpie® marker, white sticky labels and a variety of small freezer bins to corral similar items.

If you have a UFO (Unidentified Frozen Object),

toss it in the trash bin. Sort other items by category, like fruits, veggies, meat, poultry, bread, ice cream/sweet treats, pizza and leftovers.

Take this opportunity to wipe down the inside of your freezer. You may not see it again for a while!

Corral like items in a right-size container. If you have clear drawers in your freezer, see what category of items would fit nicely in each drawer.

Use deep baskets for bulky items like bread or large bags of pasta. Use medium size bins for squishy, bagged items like frozen veggies or fruit. Use tiered shelves for stacking leftovers and pizzas.

As you put things away, make an inventory list on a dry erase board and keep it on the front of your freezer. When you take something out, erase it. When you put food away, add it to the list.

Knowing exactly what you've got stashed in your freezer will save you time and money as you plan meals and shop for groceries. Step back and look at your new and improved freezer! Now *that* is organazm worthy!

HOT TIP

This is a great project for before and after pictures. Post the before picture on your freezer door for inspiration!

47.
Recipe for Success

Recipes tend to be another type of paper that can get totally out of hand! Even if you have a plethora of wonderful cookbooks sitting on your kitchen shelf, it's just so tempting to clip every yummy looking recipe you run across in newspapers or magazines or on websites.

Sadly, many of these recipes die a lonely death and never see the light of your kitchen – they just get shoved in a drawer or stacked on a counter. Even three-hole punching them and placing them in a binder doesn't guarantee that the recipe will ever be used.

There are several ways you might try to stop the madness.

1. Clear out your recipe file, stack or binder every month or so. It's amazing how a week or two of perco-

lating might change your opinion of how awesome that recipe really sounds.

2. During your meal planning time, actually peruse your recipe file, pull one out and plan to make it!

3. If you and your family aren't thrilled with the results of a particular recipe, just toss the recipe out. There are too many other wonderful recipes out there. Life's too short for "meh" recipes!

4. Create a system to store your clipped recipes by category. It can be as simple as file folders labeled "breakfast," "side dishes," "chicken," "Thai," "sweets," "salads," etc.

5. Use an online recipe clipper to keep delicious sounding recipes you find on the Internet. Don't print them out! That only adds to the paper clutter in your kitchen.

6. Too many cookbooks? Copy your favorite recipes from some of them and donate the book.

7. And, of course, you could just stop clipping recipes and use the ones you've already got!

48.
Memories

For many of us, it's our nature to want to save treasured memorabilia. These can be as simple as photos, artwork, report cards, ticket stubs or newspaper clippings. Special clothing, love letters, diaries or certificates might also have unique meaning to you.

There's nothing wrong with saving sentimental objects, but keep in mind a few simple tips when doing so.

Special items deserve a special home. Observing the "like with like" practice, use a pretty box or bin to store your sentimental artifacts. This will help keep them clean and protected from mildew, dust and water damage. Label the box clearly with the year or the decade, depending on the volume of the contents.

Use archival paper and/or boxes if you are storing one-of-a-kind documents or clothing like christening gowns, wedding gowns or baby clothes.

If you come across a treasured old photo or letter that a close friend or family member might also appreciate, copy it and pass it along to them.

Consider these boxes and bins the repositories of your own personal narrative, the story of your life so far!

49.
It's a Marathon, Not a Sprint

However much we might wish it, there will probably never come a day when we can say, "There. Now I'm organized!" It would be so lovely if it were possible! But you will likely end up banging your head against a wall, throwing up your arms and giving up if you have an unrealistic view of what you can accomplish.

In the world we live in, there is so much coming at us – paper, commitments, responsibilities, activities, information – that we must incorporate new habits and strategies to help us stay sane while keeping all the plates spinning on a daily basis.

Getting organized is not a sprint. It's not a single event. It is about changing behaviors. If you can think about the organizing process as a long-term, ongoing way of life, you will begin to see progress in the little things.

Do a little every day and preserve what you have accomplished!

50.

I'm Worth It!

You are worthy of living in an environment that feeds your soul instead of crushing it.

You are worthy of living in a home that reflects what's important in your life.

You are worthy of living in an atmosphere that allows you to relax more and stress less.

Please consider that getting your life more organized is an attainable way to reach these worthwhile goals. Once you've taken the time and energy to think about what's important in your life, set goals to mesh with those priorities and changed your behaviors to reach those goals, you will begin to feel that you are controlling your world and that you are not just a bystander letting life control you.

Yes, you are worth it!

Climax

Well, that's *50 Shades of Organizing...Your Life*! We hope that you've gleaned some gems to help make your life a little more organized. A little more relaxed. A little less stressed.

Remember that getting more organized is a process. Backsliding happens to all of us. Just keep moving forward toward your vision of how you'd like your life to look. Take care of yourself and good things will happen!

Don't forget that all of the products and resources we mention in *50 Shades of Organizing...Your Life* can be found on The Organazm Ladies' website http://www.50ShadesOfOrganizing.com. Why don't you come visit us there?

CPSIA information can be obtained
at www.ICGtesting.com
Printed in the USA
FFOW05n1258181115

9 780986 421419